BE YOUR OWN HELP

●●● developing your self-love via Confidence and good Relationships.

(Judy G. Shaw)

Table of Contents

Dedication

I dedicate this book to you for sacrificing your time and resources in pursuit of knowledge towards a healthier lifestyle.

INTRODUCTION

Self-love is an essential attribute on needs in developing oneself and appreciation of the beautiful nature of mankind. You the type that lacks the boiling desire needed to form self-assurance in yourself and creating excellent relationships with others? You often feel some bit of clumsiness with yourself and around others, maybe undue coyness. Loving yourself — knowing yourself — can help you get over these problems quickly.

Having confidence in yourself, together with the ability to relate properly with others, comes from within — knowing yourself. Everything you want to achieve has to be achieved or programmed within your mindset before it's completed. Your sense of self belief, awareness, and happiness gives you the ability to interact with confidence, thereby going on to build positive relationships.

CHAPTER ONE

THE ATTRACTIVENESS OF LOVING SELF AND MANKIND

What really gear this is the fact that loving m myself and those around me has begat a consciousness. A sense of a purpose-driven life. Take this and hold to it firmly: "Loving yourself and those around you can bring you a new lease of life than you presently have — the prospect to live with self-confidence, bond with others, and building progressive relationships."

Everything and anything that a man aims to achieve is built on his belief, love, and happiness with himself. Let this be known to us that, our day to day activities is only affected positively or negatively by how well we treat ourselves. Whatever relationships we have or build with others, our work ethics, and our desires, is a direct reflection of how we picture ourselves from within before it's shown to the outside world. It's based on the energy or life we inject into our living that we impact our environment.

Humans need every moment of self-love to meet with their core desires for success, the achievement of personal growth, and development. Self-love creates those passionate feelings, beliefs, and core desires upon which our happiness with ourselves and warmth towards others can have a foundation. The ability to be optimistic, satisfied, and acceptant of your person is down to your self-love. This self-love is the driving force you need to be steadfast and confident in relating to others. Don't you think it fit that you need to start loving yourself better than you already do? Let's take a step further. Before this further steps, let this be clear to you that the onus lays on you more because no person or individual would do it for you. At this junction you have to do it yourself.

WHAT IS SELF-LOVE?

This will be a boring task if a little analysis is not done. This is because a specific definition to this might lead or contradict your school of thought. Therefore, on this stand because the term Self-love is quite a complicated task to take on. To define or understand the idea of self-love let's look towards two key terms that characterizes it; 'Self' and 'Love' for a cue which will be in form of conceptualization. Self has to do with a particular person, his awareness, and essential nature or being that separates him from others. Love, on the other hand, has to do with the intense emotions, beliefs that arise from in-depth affection, warmth, and protectiveness towards others. With this in mind, self-love simply put, is the awareness, deep feelings of affection, care, and notice you can show to yourself. It has to do with the overall ability to show confidence and utmost care in your gifts to take care of your being. Have you ever felt this way? I mean, feeling all loved up for yourself? If yes or no is your answer to this question, let's go further and see what can be achieved with loving yourself.

Rationally, the contiguous relationship one (you) can ever have with anyone is with yourself. You remain the only one who can be there for yourself every twinkle of an eyes and during periods of agony, fun, and pleasure. That is, not to say your close friends and allies won't be there to help guide you through different difficult and rosy phases of your life. The implication of this is that they can't continually be there for you at all times. After all, they are humans just like you and have needs and interests of their own to cater to. So, on this note loving one-self is essential and important to every individual which you are. To buttress this more believe it or not all human are self-interested which connote self-love.

Structure your self-confidence levels via self-love

Let this be known to you, having confidence in yourself does not have to do with a emotion of supremacy, right, or being cocky towards others. It just has to do with being certain of yourself, knowing your and weaknesses strengths, and believing in your abilities to get things finished. Confidence has to do with the assurance you place on yourself to reach your goals, visions, and ambitions complete.

This question implies to you, so you can examine yourself. Do you, in any way, feel self-assured or a lack of it about yourself or your desires? Stay calm! Everyone has some level of confidence or a lack of it from time to time. A lack of it, though, is quite influencing, and as such, could lead to the loss of fulfilling your potentials or desires and this you need to work against and try to get yourself back to your feet. I'm about to offer some deep secret on how to unknot your confidence activate switch. This top-secret should get you started or help you put up a stronger showing of your self-confidence levels.

"KNOW THY SELF"

Humans don't get to know who they are or what they are capable of doing by merely throwing themselves into achievement when opportunities arise. Not only this, by knowing yourself you can operate your assets to help others around you, and to understand the things you will excel at which connote your vision. This will unleash you to your greatness and bring the best out of you. Mind you there is a knowledge or sensation of confidence in you that has already been put in place before possibilities appear that gives you the go-ahead to act. We already tend to know we can get things done when there is that sense of self-belief, the feeling of being comfortable within ourselves, and a feeling of self-worth. This feeling is called self-love! Believe me this self-love will unleash you to the best you have ever achieved in your career.

Without you knowing within yourself your physical, mental, emotional capabilities, it would be an arduous task getting things done. To get out of this mountain of a problem, you need to begin a search for the knowledge of yourself. Socrates, the renowned Greek philosopher, said, "Know thy self." While several literary claims and meanings have been attributed to this statement, one meaning is essential to us here. You can't be able to go through the odds, ills, pains, fun, or rosy aspects of life without an understanding of yourself. You need to draw strength from the love you have for yourself, which is drawn from "knowing you" to be able to develop that burning confidence required to push things forward. The knowledge of yourself and your abilities allows you to learn, unlearn, and relearn with confidence and ease. In a nutshell knowing yourself could be narrow to this: regarding (but not ascribing to) your assets and flaws, your desires and doubts and dreams, your views and moods, your likes and dislikes, your tolerances and limits.

Let's use this scenario, considering an example of self-assurance from a young adult who admires a woman from afar at his place of work. They are both colleagues at the same establishment for quite a while, with the only discussions between them been the customary hellos, how is work — general office work scenario. The man has been trying to summon up the courage to ask this woman out for some time but pauses at the last minute.

Days spill into weeks, and weeks into months, and months into a year, two years, and still counting. Yet the man is still trying to summon up that extra bit of courage to bring his desired result home a date and probably more. He was afraid because he has never asked a woman out in his life. During this trying period, a smart guy with an attribute of self-love got employed at this same place of work, and within a month, he asks the same lady out. Boom! Your guess is as good as mine! She agrees to go out on a date with this new guy. It's the talk among the ladies in the establishment, and our initial man who could not summon up the courage is emotionally down as a result when words reached him.

Now, let's backtrack a bit by breaking things down a little. Do you grasp that the above example shows confidence and a lack of it? The man who took quite a long time to speak his mind lacked the courage or self-love. He did not believe or love himself enough to know his weaknesses and capitalize on it with his strengths. On the other hand, the new man burns with self-awareness. It does not matter whether there is always a first time at everything, especially for the man who lacked confidence. What is of importance is that the level of self-confidence burns from knowing it's alive. It is your ability to love and know yourself before any new event that proves you capable of taking specific actions.

Being confident in yourself is structured around your ability to rely or depend on your persuasion. To be reliant and dependent on yourself to live a life brimming with confidence no matter the situation, knowing yourself (self-love) is vital. Knowing who you are allows you to create strong values and ideals around your persona. It builds up a psychological or mental foundation that can let you stand any test before yourself, obstacles, and before anybody.

CHAPTER TWO

HOW TO SHAPE YOUR SELF-ASSURANCE BY KNOWING THY SELF

Building your confidence through self-love and knowing yourself is magical and also not magical reason being all you need to do is try work on yourself and make things work for you and stop being victim of circumstance. This "magic" is the driving force that allows you to keep your heads up no matter the circumstance. Here is how to easily build your confidence by knowing yourself. By following this steps believe it you are the peak of it.

MAINTAIN YOUR PERSONA

It is one thing to create a "why" yourself; this is a question you need to ask yourself and ponder over well. The importance of this is to maintain this "why" and let your signal keep asking you this same question often as a reminder. Never build your personality to suit that of another person always use this proof as a blueprint to your stand, "no man is born with a fingerprint that match another person's own. Always know that you are unique and incomparable to another individual. Be realistic about what you want and how you want it. Set out vigorous limits or limits between what you want to have and what you don't want to.

See yourself as equivalent or improved still unique, among others. Lowering your status to considering others better than you reduces the development of yourself. Marilyn Monroe made a relating statement, "Wanting to be someone else is a waste of the person you are." Don't be wasteful with your life and its resourcefulness. On this always be yourself and stop being a tool used by others to become or achieve their goal. This self-love will let you see further than what other sees in you and project you to be. Believe it your potential will be unleash to it best if you can apply this.

SHOW YOURSELF CARE

You need to realize that you also need some pampering. Treat yourself with greatest care, and compassion, just the way you would want others to treat you, never underrate yourself based on those around you. Never let some individual determine who you are. Without you understanding yourself and building your persona around that awareness, people would take you for granted. They would paint you to be what they want and not what you want. This you need to work on by not letting some individual determine your sphere in life. Let them see their wrong notion about you by your nonchalant attitude towards your personality and making your real self-known to them.

Ensure that you place a priority on meeting your needs at all times. This is the only way you can keep on driving towards your desires with confidence. Believe it with this move, Boom! You are there

SET OUT PERSONAL BOUNDARIES FOR YOURSELF

To feel self-assured about yourself and your actions, you need to define yourself. You need to be perfect about who you are, what you stand for, your strengths, and your weaknesses. And always try to work on your weaknesses though no man is perfect. Never allow any man to be the judge or dictator of how you feel or go about your life. This is one key area knowing yourself can help you in building confidence.

Be ready to tell others no and fairly assert possession over your life. You don't have to live your life through the nose of others — hold a firm grip on the wheels of your life. Harvey Fierstein rightly said, "Never be bullied into silence. Never allow yourself to be made a victim. Accept no one's definition of your life, but define yourself." This dictum said it all never let any man use his or her lifestyle as a parameter to your stand.

STAY COMMITTED

Do you intend to go far in your journey in this life without being committed to this your stand (self-love)? No way! There is no way around it. You need to keep up a 100 percent impeccable obligation to yourself. It is your commitment to yourself that helps you easily realize when and where to help others. Remember, you can't lead others if you don't at least have an idea of the way that is, a blind man can't lead the able men and women. You need to be fervent and consistent in your self-love. There is nothing sweeter than being committed to self-love, whether it is through taking actions meant for yourself or altruistic actions for others. It is the love you get after defining and understanding yourself that you translate to your fellow man. In a way to buttress you cannot give what you don't have.

YOUR WHY SHOULD BE WELL-KNOWN

To display that internal and external self-assurance within yourself and in your relationship with others, you need to define your why. You need to know why or what purpose is your driving force. A description of this allows you to understand your worth, strengths, weaknesses — knowing who you are boosts confidence. This gives an assurance signal to other or your critics.

Try to paint a clear image of your why, your inspirations, your charge, this is exactly what you need. Napoleon Hill says, "What the mind can conceive and believe it can achieve." It's easy to believe in yourself when you know exactly why you are. Yes! Why you are and not who they wanted but your real self.

CHAPTER THREE

STRUCTURE OPTIMISTIC ASSOCIATIONS VIA SELF-LOVE

To care for or form positive relationships with others, you have to love yourself first. Many don't realize this truth until they lose their livelihood, their loving nature, and, consequently, their confidence. Yes! You can lose your self-confidence while in the pursuit of relations with others when you lack self-love. I will guide you towards understanding what is mentioned above. This has helped many in the past and using this would be an addition to the figure of those on the right path.

Man's self-assurance level is dependent on his ability to show himself some adoration once in a while. Without discovering your love for yourself, you can't precise what you don't possess — loving others here is an illusion. Although how self-love helps build confidence and positive relationship is similar — they both need self-love as a foundation — there remains differences. It's because of this reason I decided to discuss them separately.

Some people are led into believing loving yourself disrupts you from building strong and positive relationships with others. Don't make the mistake of thinking that self-love is equal or the same as selfishness. This notion is not valid, and in the real sense of it, self-helps you understand the needs, emotions, strengths, and weaknesses of others while relating with them. Don't ever feel guilty of loving or trying to love yourself.

Let's be clear on this; every human is not selfish. Instead, we are all self-interested. We cannot rule out the fact that we all pursue one important thing or the other for ourselves. Our self-interest is such that we love ourselves and want what is best for ourselves, but without trying to force others to sacrifice their benefit. A selfish person, on the other hand, wants his interest to be met even at the expense of others getting theirs.

Parker Palmer clears the air surrounding this when he says, "Self-care is never a selfish act — it is simply good stewardship of the only gift I have, the gift I was put on earth to offer others. Anytime we can listen to true self and give the care it requires, we do it not only for ourselves but for the many others whose lives we touch." Consequently, our act of loving ourselves translates to the extent in which we can love others. If you lack self-love, it would be quite a task loving or building strong relationships with others

HOW TO BUILD POSITIVE RELATIONSHIPS

Right now we have been able to identify the role self-love plays in loving mankind. It is then important that you know how to use it to build strong relationships that can stand tests.

POSITIVE RELATIONSHIPS.

LEARN TO BE APPRECIATIVE OF OTHERS

You need to go about your relationships with others with the same positivity and respect you accord yourself. Offer genuine praise and appreciation for the qualities you value in others and what they do for you. By this, they can also find value in themselves and you for being truthful to them.

Don't get so worked up discovering people's flaws

Every human by his nature is not perfect; we all strive towards the perfection of some sort. You mustn't fret about others having flaws themselves, you also do. You make mistakes just as your friend does and will always do.

Remember, showing yourself love allows you to know yourself deeper. You are exposed to your strengths and your weaknesses. This is just the same way others persona is composed — everyone has his flaws. Take everyone to heart to be just like you, and this would work wonders for your relationship.

UNDERSTAND THAT EVERYONE IS HIS OWN SELF

One key point to note here is that our knowledge and love of ourselves allows us to respect other's persona.

Everyone has his or her relative personality traits that make him unique, and this line of difference should not be invaded. When forging relationships with others do not take it upon yourself to compulsorily make them lose their self-identity. Don't try to change people unnecessarily, only if it is a necessity. The easy way to help others grow is to shun from unhealthy criticism. Rather show them how to get things done through love.

BUILD YOUR RELATIONSHIP AROUND ACTION

How do you portray your love for others, by bottling it up inside you or by showing it? Loving others is not just about emotions you feel inside you; it is about the way you act towards those you claim to love. Don't just go about feeling love for others in your relations with them. Show them you love them by being there for them, offer them companionship, advice. This can goes a long way to help you create solid relationships with others.

TIE YOUR HAPPINESS TO YOURSELF

No one can make you happy as much as you can, no matter the extent of the relationship. If you don't possess any self-love or knowledge of yourself, external factors or connections cannot make it any better. As much as you can be happy within yourself — you are your happiness. It's your happiness that can help you love others, overlook their flaws, and as a result, build strong, positive relationships.

CONCLUSION

Loving your self is of high importance — it's not an exaggeration. It's the love you have for yourself that leads to knowing you. It is this knowledge that translates the self-confidence and strong relationship built with others. Don't take for granted the significance of loving yourself within yourself and your circle of friends. This self-love is your only gateway to happiness and contentment.

The insightful, knowledgeable tips offered here are to help you scale your present difficulty feeling confident about yourself. It is based on the foundations of confidence laid by self-love that you can transfer love to others — building positive relationships. Build yourself and relationship around these hacks presented to you, and feel the positive change. I believe by so doing you will accomplish all your wishes in life.

OTHER BOOKS BY SAME AUTHOR

1. **WEIGHT LOSS WITH DR SEBI APPROACH:**
…Food and health via Dr Sebi approach.
https://kdp.amazon.com/amazon-dp-action/us/dualbookshelf.marketplacelink/B089525HYM

2. **BOOST YOUR IMMUNE SYSTEM WITH DR SEBI APPROACH**

…Food and health via Dr Sebi approach.

https://kdp.amazon.com/amazon-dp-action/us/dualbookshelf.marketplacelink/B089525HYM